Creeping and

By Liza Charlesworth

ISBN: 978-1-339-02788-3

Art Director: Tannaz Fassihi; Designer: Tanya Chernyak
Photos © Getty Images and Shutterstock.com.
Copyright © Liza Charlesworth. All rights reserved. Published by Scholastic Inc.

1 2 3 4 5 6 7 8 9 10   68   32 31 30 29 28 27 26 25 24 23

Printed in Jiaxing, China. First printing, August 2023.

■SCHOLASTIC

A big cat can creep.
See it creeping in
the thick green grass.

A big cat can leap.
See it leaping from a tree
onto a rock. Yikes!

Chomp, munch!
A big cat can eat a lot.
It's eating a hunk of meat.

Can a big cat float? Yes!
See it floating in a lake.
Big cats can swim well.

Take a peek at this!
A big cat is peeking from
its home in a stone cave.

Run, jump, hug, play!
This big cat is playing
with its cub. That is fun!

Can a big cat dream? Yes!
It's dreaming of creeping
and leaping. Zzzzzzzzz!